Merry Christmas,
        Caroline!

We certainly miss you.
Hope you enjoy our
cats!

        Randy

    12-11-05

Pavlov's Cats

ALSO BY RANDY MINNICH

Wildness in A Small Place

This book is dedicated to the people at Animal Friends of
Pittsburgh and the work they do. A portion of the purchase price
of this book will be donated to them.

R. M.

I've learned the Stations of the Tail,
Variations on Meow,
at least three Tones of Purr, and how
the Jungle gleams inside your eyes...

Pavlov's Cats

Poems

By Randy Minnich

Illustrations

By Erin Sloane

Photographs of Randy Minnich and front cover cats by Claudia Minnich
Photograph of Erin Sloane by Ethan Sloane

Book design by Cheryl Neuendorffer

ISBN 1-4116-6021-8

First Edition

Printed in the United States of America

CONTENTS

CONTENTS

ILLUSTRATIONS

Illustrator's Note:
I based each illustration on a wildflower that the poem's theme brought to mind. The flowers' names are in italics.

Foreward

Dogs were the pets of my childhood. Hunting dogs. Outdoor dogs. Dogs that lived their lives at the circumference of a round, packed-dirt world, dragging their chains behind them. I think they lived good lives, nonetheless. My brothers and I took them walking and hunting, let them run loose when we could, mourned them when they strayed onto the highway. We loved them, albeit from a distance.

Cats. They came from the neighbors' yards. We knew them as aloof, half-wild phantoms that slunk around the perimeter of our world, leaving only loose feathers drifting across the yard and sticky surprises in the sandbox.

All this became moot after I married: Claudia loved, but was allergic to dogs, cats, llamas, and just about everything else with four legs and fur. We had to love them from afar. Then we met Dusty.

Dusty was a septuagenarian—in cat years—when we moved into her neighborhood. She was the matriarch. Even in her waning years, she was a mighty hunter and dispenser of justice. Cats and dogs feared her; humans adored her. She already owned several houses on the block and was negotiating for ours. But for the allergies, we would have sold—no, given ours to her, too. We had fallen in love. Several years later, when she was about 110, she limped off into the night and disappeared. Her passing left a larger hole in our lives than we would have imagined.

At about the same time, Claudia reached a birthday that called for re-evaluations. She was going to have a pet now, or never. She reacted to all dogs, but there was this hairless hypoallergenic breed of cat, the Devon Rex, that had been bred for people like her. She decided on now. We drove to Ohio to see a lady about a cat.

Daisy was silver-gray, the runt of the litter, and the trial case for the cat kingdom. She passed, with honors. The following year, we brought her nephew, Rusty, home. Several years later, after experience and modern medicine had tamed the allergies and we had become convinced that we <u>really</u> like cats, we adopted an abandoned kitten. Tuck, we tell ourselves, fills out the family.

The poems that follow tell how these three have taught us about their species, how they have taken over the house that Dusty desired, how they've helped us understand those lost souls who can't say no—and have a hundred cats.

Thanks to the Squirrel Hill Poetry Workshop for struggling with me as I tried to find the words for "cats," to Shirley Stevens for editing all those words, to Erin Sloane for turning them into pictures, and to Cheryl and Tom Neuendorffer for transforming the manuscript into a book.

And thanks, especially, to Claudia for inspiring, reading, and critiquing the individual poems and for urging me to gather them into a story. It isn't easy to herd cats—or cat poems. Were it not for her, these would still be scattered across the house, napping.

Also, because of Claudia's particular concern for lost and abandoned pets, we have decided to thank Animal Friends, Inc. for their care and concern for such animals by donating royalties from this book to them. Animal Friends is Pittsburgh's only full-service, no-kill shelter for homeless and unwanted dogs and cats. Their mission is to provide temporary homes for animals in need, to find good, permanent homes for them, and to educate the public to reduce the animal abuse that causes the problem. They average 2,200 adoptions per year. We feel privileged to be associated with these kind and dedicated people and to be able to help support their work.

And now to the cats. Dusty's hearing, by the way, was excellent.

xx

A Conversation with a Deaf Cat

"Dusty, stay out of the garage.
This isn't your house.
I'm sorry,
you can't come in.
I'll just carry you out if you do...
See? Now go home...Dusty!
Oh don't complain; I told you:
every time that you come in,
I'll carry you back out again...
Look, the basement's cold and dirty.
Later, you'll want out, but
you'll be trapped down here.
Hey! Don't go under there!
Well, have it your way, then.
But you'll get hungry in the night.
I'll bring some water down.
No! You can't go upstairs!
Damn it, Dusty, go back down!
Aw geez. Listen. You sleep
on the rug here by the heater.
Tomorrow you go home.
No, you can't get on the bed...

Poetry on Motion

I'd thought that kittenhood
was something soft and sweet—
ah, but Teacher, now I know:
a kitten is a whirlwind loose
inside a scattered room,
nose and ears all aquiver
beneath a question-mark tail.

And if little girls
are of sugar and spice,
kittens are of razor blades
and rubber bands in velvet wrap,
ricocheting by and gone.

For when your tail is afire,
gravity stands breathless
as you leap like a top gone mad
from some mystery on the window sill,
over the mantle,
under the table,
and into a box upstairs—
in the blink of a round yellow eye.

And if you race
from daffodil to butterfly—
well, race you should
and race you must.
For springtime is an Eden
of wonders and delights,
and paws are almost wings,
but April's feet are faster still.
She'll dash away to leave the kitten
out of breath and far behind,
under August's sun,
blinking sleepily.

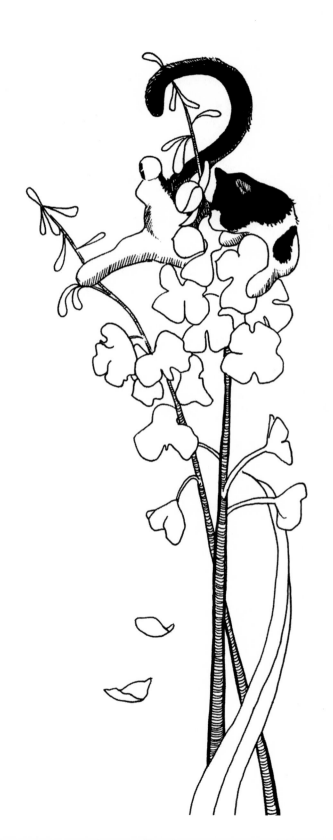

The Limits of Love

You've had all your shots
and eat only vet-approved meals.
The windows are secure,
the philodendrons gone,
from a thoroughly kitten-proofed home.

We step around you carefully,
lift you gently from the stove,
and softly speak with you
of thunderstorms and rain.

But when the sun has set,
you stalk the darkest corners
on centipede patrol, and pounce
on ants and leap for moths—
unchaperoned, you terrorize
the folk of Lilliput.

So, little one, I fear
you'll have to learn
about the hornet
from the hornet.

Spayed

It was right; the thing to do—
so everybody said.
And it's as done as yesterday
so we will smile and carry on.
Still, part of me is desolate.

Not because you walk in pain,
tail adroop and looking up
with large sad eyes
of innocence in misery—
no, the pain will pass

and you will soon forget;
live your life not knowing
lusty screeching nights,
the wild ferocity of love,
suckling kittens at your side.

No, it's the proper things we do
to others for their betterment—
like clothing jungle Indians
and saving tigers with the cage.
They pace; I acquiesce
with a hollow "Aye."

Daisy and the Whale

The whale's song must pour out
from some deep pool behind its eyes,
from that dark well of ancient waters
where the grandsires of all sounds were born:
the moonlight howls, the morning trills,
the antlered bugling of autumn.
And Brahms is just a shimmer
on the surface of that deep dark sea.

All this I learned from Daisy,
for Daisy lives upon that shore.

Oh, normally, she's curled up on a pillow
on sunny afternoons to watch
the slow suburban world drift by—
a car, a bird, a bicycle—
and soon drifts off, herself, and dozes
while human music floats above her
like wispy puffs of flimsy cloud
and she just blinks and nods.

But put urbanity aside,
switch to tape of older song:
the ballads of Leviathan
wailed and moaned beneath the sea;
then lightning strikes from a blue sky.
Eyes wide, ears up, and tail aswitch,
she leaps to seek the singer,
paws the speaker, circles it,
and mews a quiet feline counterpoint.

For though she's never seen a whale,
Daisy knows the ancient waters well,
would dive into the speaker, if she could.
That same pool lies
deep and dark behind her eyes.
I know, for I have heard the wild geese
calling in the night
and trembled on my leash.

Understanding

Like the in-breathing of dawn,
the breathing out of evening,
you've lived a year of days with me
and now I know you well:

the windows that you watch from,
the paths that lie between,
where you curl for naps—and when—
and what you have to say.

I've learned the Stations of the Tail,
Variations on Meow,
at least three Tones of Purr, and how
the Jungle gleams inside your eyes

at times. Yes, I know you well—
as well as I understand
how dawn arrives,
and where the sun sets to…

The View from Inside

Aquiver on the window ledge
as huge white flakes drift down,
you crouch with lashing tail
as all the little birds flit by
atwitter and aflutter oh so close—
they might be antelope at water
and you a lion in the grass.
"One hop more... Come on.
Just one more step and...
Oh damn that window pane!"

Lioness, did you not know
that these are children of the few
who passed through fires that laid
the other dinosaurs low?
That, nonchalant, they dance on drifts
where you would founder, first, then freeze?
Do you think those pert black eyes
know less of glass than you?
Like much out there beyond your gate,
they're not as easy as they seem.

Pantomime and Guesses

If I understood you rightly,
that barbed wire hug you wrapped
around my hand was Feline
for affection. Juliet,
at least, could speak Italian.
We must do with intonations,
pantomime, and guesses of what lies
within the dark behind strange eyes.

And trust in what is said
in all the easy ways we touch:
I haul you around,
out of and off from;
you sit on my stomach
and walk on my chest—

And I remember how you paced
all night as I lay coughing.

Cultural Differences

As I sit in the tub
washing my feet,
you look on in wonder
that someone would be
in water by choice—
and you shudder.

You have a better way with yours:
sit in the sun on a pillow
and lick them. Yet I watch
your tongue slip blithely
over claws like broken glass—
and I cringe.

Just a Guess

So I said to the one-eyed man
with just three fingers
on one hand,
"When did you bring the kitten home?"

He froze me in his one-lamp glare,
then hissed through lips
with a ragged tear,
"A month ago. How did you know?"

The Tao of a Leaky Faucet

Though just a trickle in the sink,
it stops the kitten in mid-bounce
to puzzle, as on tea-leaves or a ball:
it leaps, as he did, out of darkness
into a wide-eyed world,
sparkles for a moment in the sun,
and as a gray old cat,
disappears into the night.

Perplexed, he peers into the drain,
sniffs the rising dampness—
the streamlet dribbles off his ear.
He jingles as he shakes fine spray,
pats with a tentative paw
the thread of silver droplets,
draws back, sits down,
head cocked, and watches.

At last he bows
to one more of Life's mysteries—
and drinks it.

Rusty's Race for Freedom

The door to Outside
was slightly ajar:
a thin black crack
in his bright warm world.

His two yellow eyes
peered cautiously out:
two thin black slits
staring into One.

It called. He leaped.
But two bounds into
the cold wet night—
Rusty reconsidered.

Trust

Curled up on my lap
she lays a paw full of knives
in velvet sheaths
softly on my wrist.

Times twenty of her,
I must loom huge,
my heavy hand behind her—
but only lest she fall. And so

we doze together in the sun.

Daisy Reads the News

She's been napping in the western sun
upstairs all afternoon.
Now the sun is down, and so is she:
stalks silently into the living room,
sniffs the weather on my hat,
on my shoes the passages of all the critters
whose pathways cross the yard,
the family's travels in the coat closet,
and, though it's quite invisible to me,
some editorial on the rug.
Then, satisfied that all is well,
stretches long and deep,
hops lightly to my lap,
curls up and falls asleep.

Daisy and the Telephone

For Daisy, the telephone
is a puzzle and a trial:
"What is this shrill thing?
It's cold and hard,
can't cuddle or purr,
but they run to it
and talk to it—
treat it like a cat.
Better, sometimes."

Genes hammered out
on dark jungle nights
gave her fingers too stubby
to grasp a phone.

Her puzzlement comforts me
when <u>my</u> mysteries
haunt the hollow hours:
How can this deep black sky
go on and on and on?
What's beyond the universe?
How can forever—be?
How can I not—some day?

It's good, then,
to remember Daisy.
The world is too big
for my genes, too.

The Hairless Cat

Her tongue runs roughly over
taut cords and a soft pink belly
that ought to be bundled
in thick proud fur. But no,
we've juggled her genes
lest we sneeze, wrapped her instead
in a house. Left her too fragile
to stalk plump doves in the snow.

No matter. She prowls the midnight halls
as huge and gray as a high ridge cougar,
twin shoulder blades carving the darkness,
eyes of wild green fire.

And as she drowses in the sun,
a leopard draped on a limb of chintz
above the slow suburban stream,
I finally understand:
wildness is a state of mind.

Demise of a Half-eaten Pumpkin Pie

We'll never know if it was boredom
or the seductive smell of spice.

We do know we heard a busy scritch-scratch,
a splat and a crash.

And there on the counter stood Rusty,
tail high, peering over the edge,

with a half-smile revealing
no trace of chagrin,

but rather an air of amused satisfaction—
and one ear cocked pragmatically back

toward the hurrying feet in the hall,
and the approaching storm.

The Travels of an Indoor Cat

I slogged in the mud among
green skunk cabbage stalks,
scuffed through the leaf-duff
where sow bugs and millipedes dwell,
stepped fairly carefully over the pellets
the white-tailed deer had dropped,
then ambled happily home
across the young spring grass.

My boots I place,
most carefully now,
on a newspaper in the sun
so when Rusty snuffs
for the distilled essence of woods,
he can get out, too.

A Close Encounter of the Feline Kind

Attila sits brazenly on the porch step,
insolently appraising,
through the screen,
the decadence of Rome.

Inside,

peering over the parapet,
Rusty glares back.
His tail switches wildly.
He yowls and huffs and paces

until I slam the window shut—
bang—and the Hun slips smoothly
and coolly away. Then
Rusty lifts his right rear leg

to begin his bath.

A Stroke of Lightning

It was close and loud,
with a promise of more.
Suddenly, Daisy arrived:
low and fast,
her tail straight out behind.

"Don't worry," I said. "It's ok.
Crawl under the blanket with us."

She looked up at me,
then at the tangle of blankets and legs.
Looked out the window
at the dark, rumbling sky,
once more at me,
and dove under the bed.

A Balance of Power

Rusty lies in cozy places—
a lap or a dollop of sunshine—
an ocher and white ball of fluff
blinking placidly—
most of the time.

But once in the morning,
once in the afternoon,
he unrolls his domesticated plush
to stretch the long hard frame underneath,
uncoils two fistfuls of razor-sharp blades,
and yawns hugely, nonchalantly,
crocodilian.

Or on a sudden inspiration, leaps
to lay waste to a sofa or chair.
Then looks up, unblinking, at me,
just to remind me who
I'm hauling off couches
and driving to the vet.

So once or twice a week—
when I'm sure that he's watching—
I stomp a milk jug to rubble,
toss it casually into the trash,
and gaze down at him, unblinking,
to help him maintain some perspective.

Tuck Meets the World

One day, the big man hauled him
out of the warm box, shoved him
into a cold one he couldn't see out of.
After a rumbly kind of time, the man grabbed him
by the neck, tossed him
into some tall grass, and left.

Tuck didn't know the way home, so
he just crawled under a bush.
Rain fell.
It got dark, and the trees all around
made scary sounds.
He cried sometimes.
He shivered a lot.

When it got light again,
he was hungry, too.
He still cried, sometimes. And once
when he cried, a big black dog
stuck its nose in his face and
its lady picked him up,
put him gently in her pocket.

She left him in a big room that smelled funny.
Nobody came in there much.
But there was food in a bowl, and water,
a big chair, and a blanket on the floor.
When the lady did come in,
Tuck ran under the chair.

After a lot of days, two new people came in.
The lady made soft sounds;
the man wiggled a string on his shoe.
It was an exciting kind of string, so
Tuck came out from under the chair
to catch it. Sometimes he did, but
it always got away. And then
the lady picked him up—from underneath—
and cuddled him.

They put him in another box—
this one had holes to look out of—
and there was another rumbly time. And now
he's curled up in the lady's lap
in a new house. There's food in a bowl
in the corner, and water, and a ball.
It's warm and he's sleepy,
so he makes his own rumbly time.

And Tuck supposes
that this was the way
it was meant to be
all along.

The Kitten's Despair

Just when you've found a spot
of sunshine on the rug,
rolled the world
into a furry placid ball,
there's this fuzzy black thing
flipping in your face.

Well, of course you have to catch it—
discipline's at stake—
but the rascal's really agile—
quicker than a catnip rat—
always just an inch ahead
and nipping at your butt.

You snap, you growl,
your feet are but a blur.
You have to stop this insolence.
Old Fuzz floats, taunting,
still a whisker past your nose.

But lest you turn to butter
as Sambo's tigers did,
you give it up at last,
flop panting to the floor.

Then, just as your sluggard breath
is finally catching up,
there's that fuzzy fellow
in your face again.
Oh, the drudgery of twirling!

Tuck's Soliloquy

"It's been a good morning.
Raced Rusty down the stairs,
listened to the people yell
'Who fell?' Played Figure Eights
between the big man's feet, watched
him open up a can, nibbled
at some chicken bits, watched
Daisy heave a hair ball, then
watched the scrubbing of the rug. Took
the sink plug out, played hockey
with it for a while, watched
the man look all around for it.
Tackled Rusty, bit his tail, and rolled
around until the people yelled,
'Stop that!' What a day!
And in just a couple of hours,
the sun will come up!"

A Matriarch's Promise

Daisy used to fly
mattress to mantle
as lightning leaps the sky.

Now, though, she prefers
to lie couchant in the house's
hot exhalations
making up riddles.

So when Tuck rockets by,
ears laid back,
eyes round and wild
with youth's octane—
and locked upon her
twitching tail—

she reminds him she's agreed,
if he'll leave her alone,
he can live
his whole life
with a nose.

A Grand Unified Theory

As cold November rain streams down
the window panes, I curl
around a treatise called "The Search
for Reality". That tome lies darker
in my hands than the stormy night
upon the land. I grope
through its pages for analogies
for particle duality or a glimmer
of what time might be. Suddenly

Daisy leaps rumbling to my lap,
sits directly in the middle of the Aspect test
of non-locality, fills my universe
with great gold eyes, blows cold kisses
up my nose, says "Pet me now!"
Layers of abstraction peel away.
There is one absolute, one point
from which the galaxies are fleeing.
Her name is Daisy!

Lightning flashes in the night.
I realize at last that Einstein's
"spooky action at a distance"
is only Daisy, instantly appearing
at the faintest crumbling of a cracker.

    What a shame.
We could have had a theory of everything
so many years ago,
had Schroedinger been nicer to his cat.

Body Language

Some find cats inscrutable,
"Meow" an empty phrase.

But on the windowsill sits Tuck,
ears forward, tail twitching—
"A chipmunk's in the flowerbed."

I walk by, followed by his ears—
"What's up?" they wonder.
I scratch his chin,
the tail goes up,
wraps around my arm—
"I like you, too." And later,

ears watching me, claws
upon the corner of the couch—
"Stop that!" I shout.
He walks away,
tail high, nose, too—
"Hmph. And who elected you?"

Ears back, tail switching, Daisy watches,
eyes wide yellow-green windows—
"He gets too much attention."

If You've Seen One Cat...

The cats were curled
like leopard spots
in a golden ring
the sunlight cast,

when gravity called
the mug rack home.
Crockery crashed.
Shrapnel flew.

Tuck raced to investigate,
Daisy just slept on,
and we didn't see Rusty
for days.

On Impressing a Cat

Rusty's perched on the sink,
monitoring my shave.
I scrape the last stubble,
wash my face, and sigh,
"Now I feel more human."

Two thin black slits
gaze coolly at me
and through to the ceiling above.

He stands, stretches,
hops to the floor,
and swaggers away.

I'd do better, he thinks,
to leave the whiskers
and feel more feline.

You think too much
Zorba the Greek

I once knew an astronomer
who gazed into the void
too long.
One starry night he put
a bullet through his head.
He should have had a cat.

For on my empty nights
when the infinite is perched
like a great black bird
upon my chest,
Tuck's wisdom chases it away.

Tuck doesn't read.
Thinks a book's
a pleasant place
to sit.

He can't fathom calculus.
Can't integrate trajectories
to calculate the point
where pounce and mouse
should intersect.

He gets there, though,
nonchalant and purring.

You Are What You Watch

Tuck watches TV.
He sits, ears forward, staring
at the window in the box
with nothing behind it.

He likes that Australian guy
with all the snakes,
figure skaters
flitting around,
and the birds that chirp
during "golf."
But he likes the cat shows best—
especially the lions.

You Don't Hang Up on Daisy

The phone rings at dinner.
A voice I've never heard asks
"How are you tonight, Mr. Minsh?"
I answer, "Click."
The TV news that droned behind me
blares into a Message—
another click. I'm free again.

But I'll be undone
if the advertisers ever make
a deal with Daisy.
She'll stand on my lap
kneading with paws
that are only as sharp
as they need to be,
gaze up through round yellow eyes,
and purr softly,
"GM trucks."

Cats' Ears

Sometimes I envy cats' ears.
Daisy hears crackers snap
three rooms and an afghan away.
At midnight, Tuck
hears millipedes
tiptoeing up the wall.

Rusty seems soundly asleep in the sun…
his ears, though, flutter and swivel
to follow each sound in the room.
And that's why cats' ears
won't do for me.

At dinner with my wife,
my right one attends
to her every word—
the left strays off to spy
on a couple's soft words
at a table nearby.

At a sports bar, laid back
on my hackles
they betray my opinion,
despite my bland smile,
as the President speaks on TV.

No, such ears would be a burden.
Though they'd be an asset,
technically,
you can't be correct,
politically,
if your ears can't lie.

Feline Physics

Youngest of the pride,
Tuck's chore is testing
gravity. All in all,
he's pleased with it.

He's found
that rings and pills,
pencils and grapes
on the table top
tumble
off
quite
properly.

But it doesn't work
on everything:
birds and squirrels
just play with it.

Seven feet up,
in the gap between
bookcase and armoire,
it works
on round
old Rusty
but not—
so far—
on Tuck.

Poor Old Rusty

Your life is a drag:
hauling that belly
from east to west
across the plush rug
as the sun slides away—

Some practice piano,
I practice sarcasm
on cats.
If my tone is sweet
they seem to enjoy it.

Today, in the shower,
I found near my navel
an unexplained scratch—
the price, perhaps,
of being sarcastic
to cats.

Castaways

Treetops sweep a wild gray sky.
A restless sphinx on a quilt-tossed bed,
Tuck flinches as leaves flit by,
ears flicker as cold hard rain
flings itself at his window pane.

He could have been the other one:
the kitten, newly abandoned,
curled beneath a thorn bush
in the dim November sun.
He might have spurned my offerings,
slipped silently into the meadow grass
and disappeared. He could be slinking
frightened and famished in the night,
quaking when the wild dogs howl,
cowering under the owl's mute wings.

He knows. He turns
from the window, grooms my arm
with his nail-file tongue,
holds me still with a cotton paw,
with a silky shoulder dries me.

The Gray Cat

We finally caught the gray cat:
the terror of the meadow,
the shadow that flowed
through the grasses.

She glares from the trap,
bristles and hisses
at treats and soft words—
all she wants
is an open door.

Dumped, years ago,
by the roadside to die,
she survived
the first wild nights,
grew terrible and sly,
stalked little creatures
in fierce solitude,
ate and was not eaten.

But this field is a haven
for bluebirds, warblers,
and others displaced
by highways and lawns.
She can't live here.

One younger, or meeker,
might find a new home,
might purr by a window someday,
become Fluffy or Tiger or Tuck.
But what house could hold
her savage soul now?
Her future is likely
a needle,
then the nap
of no awakening.

On the Gray Cat

I prefer to let poems speak for themselves. However, readers' comments have convinced me that the gray cat's story is an exception. Some haven't understood why anyone would trap this cat in the first place. The question deserves an answer.

The poem takes place in a nature preserve. Like most preserves, it has two major goals: to educate the human population about the natural world and to protect a bit of that world for its inhabitants and the future.

Of course, "protected" land still has its hazards. There is, and should be, a level of natural predation. The area in this story has resident foxes, owls, hawks, raccoons, weasels, skunks, red squirrels, and other small mammalian predators. It is also visited by several coyotes and, rumor has it, an occasional bear. The nature center's apparent placidity is deceptive. Nonetheless, the continual business of eating and being eaten is the natural way, and the populations seem pretty stable.

I don't suppose that one or two feral cats added to that list of predators would upset the balance. However, lazy and callous humans also use this area as a place to dump unwanted kittens. In one recent year, the nature center's biologist captured between fifty and sixty feral cats. Since some were pregnant, the final tally was a little over a hundred cats. The area simply can't support that many extra predators. Hence the program to capture the cats.

They aren't simply killed and that's the end of it. The biologist at the center finds homes for as many as she can. She was able to place all but five of that hundred or so. Even the remaining five weren't summarily euthanized. They were sent to a "court of last resort," a group that tries, one last time, to find homes for the really difficult cases. The gray cat went there. I don't know how she fared. It seems likely that she was too wild to place and was "put to sleep" or whatever palatable phrase you prefer for a thoroughly undeserved death.

I hoped to capture the irony of her tale and, also, a sense of the tragic and impossible choices we sometimes must make. Sometimes, something will die—in this case, the cat or her prey. The question isn't whether, it's which; and we must decide.

Tuck Watches Too Much TV

Between naps and mad moments
of ricocheting
wall to wall,
there's wrestling with Rusty,
watching over the neighborhood,
inspecting everything new—
you'd think he has a lot to do.

But no. There he lies,
a mound of fur on the couch,
licking himself
as he stalks
savannahs and jungles
on Animal Planet TV.
He blames it on me.

"I'm a hunter," he says,
"going soft in a middle class cage
with a chipmunk on the feeder
flipping his tail,
a sparrow sassing on the sill.
So let me be or let me out—
or better,

let them in."

Cats!

Two on the sink
peering down,
one in the tub
gazing up.
Barely enough
to direct
a man's shave.

Tuck Tells Time

Hawkings, Kant,
nor Einstein, nor Godel:
Is time an illusion?
Another direction?
Newtonian flow?
Platonic ideal?

I throw up my hands.
Not Tuck. He leaps
into my lap.
"It's now," says he.
"Here I am."

"Never" Means "Not Now"

Rusty is a relativist.
I tend to absolutes.

"Never eat bouquets,
especially on the mantle."

"Don't quarrel on the quilt
with Daisy while we sleep."

"No sharpening of claws
on the corner of the couch."

Mortified
by my reminders,
he slinks away,
long and low,
ears slicked back.

When I've returned
to my affairs,
he returns to his.

Golf—for Cats

Tuck is shoulder deep
beneath the couch.
Four curved claws
strain into the dusty darkness,
click against the ping-pong ball,
curl into a steely fist.

The quarry simply spins,
retreats a quarter inch.
Tuck retreats as well,
yawns and stretches,
trots away, tail high.

A ball is hard to grasp
without a thumb.
No matter. The fun
is whacking it
out of reach.

Room for Improvement

Hot water in the sink,
soap and razor set beside:
I'm ready now.

Tuck sits nearby,
ears aimed at me.
Peers into the water,
up into my face.

"Why not let them grow?
Perhaps they'll come out
sideways
so you won't bump things
when it's dark."

Greta Garbo was a Cat

Tuck and I are talking,
stretched out on the carpet
at the sunshine shore.

He's sprawled on his back,
forepaws caressing the dream
of a half-remembered mom,
rear paws gently
pressing my arm.
The tip of his tail taps
a soft slow beat,
his belly throbs
with organ chords
in D minor.

Abruptly he flips,
takes a swipe at Daisy
as she hastens by,
rolls over again.

"Where were we? Oh yes.
I'm in a book.
I'll be famous,
like Greta—
what's-her-name.
Weren't you scratching
my chin?"

Pavlov's Cats

Pavlov's cats,
I've been told,
salivated
when they damn well
pleased.